Too Bad

Sketches Toward a Self-Portrait

ROBERT KROETSCH

Too Bad

Sketches Toward a Self-Portrait

THE UNIVERSITY OF ALBERTA PRESS

Published by

The University of Alberta Press
Ring House 2
Edmonton, Alberta, Canada T6G 2E1
www.uap.ualberta.ca

Copyright © 2010 Robert Kroetsch

LIBRARY AND ARCHIVES CANADA CATALOGUING IN PUBLICATION

Kroetsch, Robert, 1927–
   Too bad : sketches toward a self-portrait / Robert Kroetsch.

(cuRRents)
Poems.
ISBN 978-0-88864-537-1

   1. Kroetsch, Robert, 1927– —Poetry.
I. Title. II. Series: Currents (Edmonton, Alta.)

PS8521.R7T66 2010   C811'.54   C2009-906592-4

First edition, second printing, 2011.
Printed and bound in Canada by Houghton Boston Printers, Saskatoon, Saskatchewan.
Copyediting and Proofreading by Peter Midgley.

A volume in *(cuRRents)*, a Canadian literature series.
Jonathan Hart, series editor.

All rights reserved. No part of this publication may be produced, stored in a retrieval system, or transmitted in any form or by any means (electronic, mechanical, photocopying, recording, or otherwise) without prior written consent. Contact the University of Alberta Press for further details.

The University of Alberta Press is committed to protecting our natural environment. As part of our efforts, this book is printed on Enviro Paper: it contains 100% post-consumer recycled fibres and is acid- and chlorine-free.

The University of Alberta Press gratefully acknowledges the support received for its publishing program from The Canada Council for the Arts. The University of Alberta Press also gratefully acknowledges the financial support of the Government of Canada through the Canada Book Fund (CBF) and the Government of Alberta through the Alberta Multimedia Development Fund (AMDF) for its publishing activities.

for Dawne and Laura and Meg and Mike

A thank you: I especially want to thank St. John's College, University of Manitoba, for giving me a supportive community in which to write these poems.

A disclaimer: This book is not an autobiography. It is a gesture toward a self-portrait, which I take to be quite a different kettle of fish.

RK

...time exists not by itself, but from actual things comes a feeling, what was brought to a close in time past, then what is present now, and further what is going to be hereafter.
—LUCRETIUS

I've kept my grandfather's axe and used it all these years. I've had to change the head twice and the handle three times.
—ANON. [courtesy of Dennis Cooley]

Contents

2   On Tour
3   Afterthought 1
4   Pirate Story
5   Afterthought 2
6   Comic Book
7   Ancestors 1: On Standing Upright
8   A Plain Lie 1
9   A Plain Lie 2
10 Emily Carr as Totem
11 Keyed In
12 Fable
13 Ancestors 2: Hoofing It
14 Classical Mythology
15 Rendezvous
16 Wild Turkeys
17 Game Theory
18 Taste
19 Wrightsville Beach, North Carolina
20 Mirror
21 For Kristian, for Assurances
22 Muse Report
23 Trade Off
24 Sage Hill Writers at St. Michael's Retreat, Saskatchewan
25 Sharing a Pizza
26 Cheticamp, Cape Breton Island
27 Guesswork
28 Just Be Yourself 1
29 Just Be Yourself 2
30 Touch
31 Winter Parka
32 Appalachian Back Roads

33	Hot Fudge Sundae
34	Making Faces
35	Driving to the Airport at Five AM
36	Just for Once
37	Please Post
38	Arctic Miracle
39	Night Vision
40	To Eli Mandel
41	CJCA, Alberta, 1935
42	Horse's Petunia
43	Pembina Highway, Winnipeg
44	Dear Mark Twain—
45	Flooding the Rink
46	If I Were You
47	NATION IN PERIL
48	Freedom of Choice: Pie Shop
49	*Anne of Green Gables*, Found Poem
50	Wind Chill Factor
51	About the Author
52	Goose Air Base, USAF
53	I Swear I Didn't Do It
54	Bad Timing
55	Country Boy
56	Walking Backwards in a Blizzard
57	I Saw It With My Own Eyes
58	The Word Sprang to My Lips
59	Visit to Japan
60	Cottage Season
61	"no ideas but in things"
62	Seduction Attempt 1
63	Seduction Attempt 2
64	Applause
65	Pessoa and His Heteronyms
66	Cars Whizzing By
67	Henri Rousseau, "The Sleeping Gypsy"

68	Terracotta Army
69	Laundering the Poem
70	Dear Lovelorn,
71	Horoscope
72	Café au Lait and Croissants in Strasbourg
73	Daedalus
74	The Feet of the Lone Traveller
75	Living Life as a Poet
76	Don't Blame Us
77	Victorian Lit, University of Alberta, 1946
78	I Try to Steal My Identity
79	Playing Cards With My Sisters
80	Nature Buff
81	My Windshield Scraper
82	Locating Story
83	Late Breaking News
84	Making an Impression
85	Cockadoodledoo
86	Watching for Signs
87	About Poetic Despair
88	About Poetic Hope
89	Grade Ten Typing Lesson: how now brown cow
90	The Sky is Falling
91	Everything Considered
92	Time to Spare
93	The Unnameable
94	Motion Sickness
95	Noosa Heads, Queensland
96	Risking It

On Tour

When the radio host said, Now tell us again
who you are, I knew I was in trouble.
Flesh become flesh, I said. I was just guessing.

I could see he was disappointed. I'll get you a printout,
I said, of my DNA. I was clutching at straws.
My dentist will have on file some X-rays.

He looked disappointed again, my radio host. I'm a cousin,
I said, to the chimpanzee, with whom you might be
familiar. He glanced at the clock on the studio wall.

You have written a book, he prompted, despairing.
Yes and no, I said. Who is it, or what, writes the book?
Maybe I'm just a transmitter.

He felt better. I was talking radio talk. You must rush out
and buy this new volume, he said. Not to me. To his listeners.
As for himself, he said, he wasn't much of a reader.

Afterthought 1

At last, winter is falling upon us, snow
rides the down elevator from invisible skies.
Now ain't this something grand?

We welcome winter. Snow is the real thing,
after the false exuberance of summer.
The first snow is soft and warm. Mothering.

I was born in the month of June.
June is a month of rainbows.
The crops were rising green.

My mother claimed I bit her nipples
so hard she couldn't breast feed.
Back then I was greedy for life.

Pirate Story

My father was wrecking an old prairie house
to salvage the lumber. He looked like a pirate,
up there on the roof ridge, swinging a hammer.

I made a sword from a plastering lath.
The gold I stole from the Spanish
was the gold they stole from the Incas.

We were in cahoots, my father and I,
he attacking the weathered house,
I attacking the ship he rode.

My sword was two-edged. My father
looked like a pirate. What does the son
of a pirate do, after the ship is demolished?

Afterthought 2

A tree is a kind of calendar, our teacher
explained, each ring in the wood a year,
each tree a memory of itself, a history

of the place and time of its growing.
Our teacher said we might bring
a sample to class. I was a good student.

My father's favourite tree was a Manitoba maple.
It stood at the edge of our garden.
It gave him shade on hot summer days.

What I did was, I cut down my father's
favourite tree. With a handsaw.
Then I cut off a slice from the fallen trunk.

The rings in the wood were a wonder.
I counted the rings. I went and told my father,
You are the same age as a tree.

My father said, Where did you find that
slice of wood? I was proud of myself.
That tree at the edge of the garden, I said.

I wasn't lying. He could see the evidence
for himself. If he wanted to. I asked him
to help me check my counting.

A tree is a kind of calendar. I remember
my father, after a moment, managed to smile.
He taught me that love has many seasons.

Comic Book

Death is a small intruder. He is painted red.
Yes, he is male. Look at the extended scrotum
(it's the heat), balls the size of avocados.

He has webbed feet (evolution gone haywire),
six fingers on each hand, but no thumbs.
The poet bpNichol might call him St. Ark.

I found the comic book in a secondhand store
in a back street in Amsterdam. I was hoping for
a forgotten portrait by Van Gogh.

No, Death is not the devil. He is an oil baron,
or possibly an investment consultant. Or a
politician from Ottawa or Washington, DC.

Or a suicide bomber in Baghdad. Or a car
accident. Or a tsunami. Or a spot
on a lung. Or a burger with fries.

The possibilities are endless. Death
likes visions of himself. He hates the simple truth.
He prefers the visions of painters and poets.

Ancestors 1: On Standing Upright

Why stand on our own two feet
when it makes more sense to run on four legs?
Our backs ache. We topple over.

We must have stood up so that we could talk.
Standing up we could learn to mouth words.
We could tell stories. We could whisper in the dark.

We could entreat the invisible gods.
We could drive an elephant over a cliff.
We could praise and console. And scold and curse.

Standing up we could make stone tools.
We could knock each other into dying.
We could use our hands to cover our ears.

A Plain Lie 1

This is a plain lie. Please read on.
Lies are necessary and unavoidable.
Consider the time I stole an apple.

I gave it to my girlfriend. She said her name
was Evie. Try this on for size, Evie, I said.
We were at a fruit stand near Vernon, BC.

What do you mean? she asked, I can never
understand you. We had only just met. It was
our first date. The sun hurt our eyes.

She polished the apple on her thigh.
I named the variety. It's an Ambrosia, I said.
The apple shone red in the sunlight.

Evie was naked. I was wearing a fig leaf because
I was standing erect. We were posing for an artist.
The artist said, Put some life into it. Move. Act.

Evie gave the apple to the artist. Bite it, she said.
You'll feel better. The artist took the apple
and ate the whole thing. He got deathly ill.

A Plain Lie 2

This Greek guy, Odysseus, said he couldn't swim.
We were in shallow water on an island in the Aegean,
showing off for some girls on the beach.

It was a nude beach. I was getting a hard-on.
I'm embarrassed, I said. Let's hit the deep water.
Deep water be diddled, Odysseus said.

That's when he told me he couldn't swim.
I knew he was lying. I knew Odysseus was a sucker
for eloquent women. He was showing off

his equipment. Like maybe he was a hero. The girls
on the beach were calling and waving him in
to the shore. I was left alone hearing voices.

Emily Carr as Totem

Emily Carr kept a pet monkey. That way
she showed us her wisdom: we are,
all of us, wisely, on a fool's errand.

It's a matter of cutting the tree down,
then carving the dead tree back to life,
totemic of what was and what might be.

She showed us by keeping a monkey:
we must learn to ascend the felled tree,
wisely, daring to be foolish.

Keyed In

Consider this key I keep on my key chain.
I can't remember what door it opened.
I can't discard the key.

Maybe it opened the door to the cupboard
in which I kept my life story.
Where did that cupboard get to?

Maybe it fit the door of that old Chev
I drove away in when I left home.
Why didn't I keep a key to the house?

But maybe it is a key to the house.
Too bad the house is gone.
It's still the place where I live.

Fable

We are the animals who talk the fables
in which the animals talk. We are talking
animals, claiming that animals don't talk.

A dinosaur and a dodo and a man
walk into this bar. The bartender asks for ID.
I forget the rest of the story.

Ancestors 2: Hoofing It

It was our walking that found the world.
Bipedal us, scavenging after lion and bear.
cracking abandoned bones for marrow,

cracking abandoned skulls for brain,
seeking seeds, insects, the eggs of nesting birds—
we walked the world round. Sorry, Magellan.

We are the keepers of the travel gene.
The ice caps drained the oceans low.
We found whole continents with our feet.

Now we arrive at land's end, wondering.
There's still a chance that we might
fall off. We are at land's end.

Classical Mythology

He dressed as a country & western singer.
He bought himself boots and a belt and a hat.
He bought an old Buick and painted it black.

He changed his name. He worked small bars
on the prairies, looking for what he'd lost.
He sang hurtin' songs that made people cry.

The woman in the Rope & Ride Saloon
was alone, drinking rye and ginger, paying
little attention. There wasn't a tear in her eyes.

He knew that she was the one. He sang her
an invitation. She smiled. Orpheus, she said.
Still up to your old tricks, I see. Keep trying.

Rendezvous

I bet my life on a poem. It was a Tuesday morning.
The sun, as usual, had seemed to come up,
though we all know it's the earth turning

on its axis that creates the illusion. We all know
that Tuesday is a name we give to a day
in a nameless sequence of nameless days.

It was a Tuesday morning and I was lolling in bed.
I had a plane to catch. I had realized, when
the hotel clerk called, that Tuesday is an illusion.

I thought of blaming the Sumerians,
for dividing the moon's light into quarters,
for inventing the minute and the hour.

I wondered about the Gregorian calendar.
How can it pretend to measure, so neatly,
our wobbly dance with a speeding sun?

I was in a city strange to me. I was scheduled
to fly to another strange city, two time zones away,
another of our illusions. The time zones, I mean.

As for the flight itself, I missed it, enough said.
I decided to apologize by writing you this poem.
Some poets claim they can transcend time.

Wild Turkeys

How do you write a poem about forgetting?
Just this morning, for instance, I walked the dog.
We saw some wild turkeys down by the river.

Or was that yesterday? I can't remember.
I'm certain I walked the dog. I'm certain
we saw the turkeys. Or was that two days ago?

If we didn't forget we'd be buried
in information. The brain is a skilled forgetter.
How else to accomplish peace of mind?

But to get back to the dog and the turkeys.
This morning I read in the *Free Press*
that one of our soldiers died in Afghanistan.

I didn't know the soldier. I have never seen
Afghanistan. The soldier was young, a son,
a husband, a father. I remember the details.

The brain is a skilled forgetter. Tomorrow morning
I'll walk the dog again. I must take special note
of the wild turkeys. I will probably forget.

Game Theory

It must be October. I was watching a hockey game,
a baseball game and a football game at the same time,
drinking a beer and munching mixed nuts.

Things were bad. The Calgary Flames were two goals down.
The Tampa Bay Rays were just about out of the running.
My Blue Bombers were losing. My beer can was empty.

Life is cruel. What could I do but switch channels again?
I chanced on a show on the building of Rome's Coliseum.
Death as a contest. Ravenous lions. Bring your own dagger.

I switched still again. Naked women eating live worms,
naked men swimming with sharks and monsoons,
a camera crew in attendance, the director out of sight.

An ad came on. For a wang stiffener. Do not use this product
if suffering from a heart condition. If you stay erect
for more than four hours, please call this TV station at once.

Taste

When my mother was impatient with me
she called me RPK. RPK, she said, Leave
those cookies alone. They're for the threshers.

I stole three macaroons and a jam-jam
and ran from the house. I had a place where
I liked to hide. It was in the shelter belt.

I knew my mother knew the place. That's why
I went there. I wanted her to come find me.
I waited. I could hear the threshers unhitching

their teams of horses, coming in for supper.
I waited and I waited. I ate the cookies.
I couldn't name the taste. I'm still waiting.

Wrightsville Beach, North Carolina

My then mother-in-law in North Carolina
introduced me to her tea-time group
as a full-blooded German. I realized

immediately that my tribal connection
gave me status. Some of the ladies
crossed their legs. Some didn't.

I should have told them my grandparents,
homesteading in Alberta, took land
away from the Cree. They had guns,

the Cree; they had hunting rifles, but
the buffalo had all been killed off.
My tribe had plows and livestock.

We had bags of seed and Treaty Six
and—what for the Cree was—
a brand-new sense of ownership.

I should have said to the ladies, We
Germanic tribes are a nasty bunch, aren't we?
Instead I said, Thank you, I'll have a cup.

Mirror

It was the improvements in mirrors that improved
the portraits of self. Titian as an old man.
Rembrandt over and over. Schiele masturbating.

How would you paint your image while dying?
How would you teach others to copy your self-portrait?
How would you paint your image while wacking off?

The glass turns your right hand into your left.
You will be judged nevertheless. Maybe you should,
like Albrecht Dürer, dress up as an Italian dandy.

For Kristian, for Assurances

I answered the young poet's question: I'm writing
short poems these days. Somehow I can't turn the pages.
Sometimes, he assured me, pages can be heavy.

I asked the young poet straight out: Why write
so much as a single poem, a single line?
Sometimes, he assured me, words need words.

Muse Report

She saw I was slow on my feet.
My iambs weren't jumpy or neat.
My choices weren't all that discreet.

She said I was heavy of heart.
I said until death do us part.
How tell the horse from the cart?

She said now isn't that tough?
Your stresses are making me puff.
Go back to keeping it rough.

Trade Off

One winter when I was a boy I went out hunting rabbits.
Rabbits were at the height of their cycle.
I had the idea that I'd buy new skates.

Rabbits were everywhere. All the boys in the country,
it seems, wanted to buy new skates. We got ten cents
for each rabbit skin. I shot eight rabbits that winter.

Supply and demand, I later learned at the U of A,
determine the price of rabbit skins. Out hunting rabbits
that winter, I learned that I liked the ice in my eyebrows,

the whisper of moccasins in snow, the stealth,
the closed eye, the beaded sight, the held breath.
I liked when I shot at a rabbit and missed.

Sage Hill Writers at St. Michael's Retreat, Saskatchewan

This is what an idyll must be (no pun intended).
The gophers in their holes (better acoustics?)
in the lawns around this hillside Retreat

listen to our poems (well, let's say they do)
and hope for cheese and cracker crumbs.
("Please keep doors closed to keep out rodents.")

At four-thirty we break out the booze. We've been
in our cells all afternoon, changing our plot lines
(the Qu'Appelle Valley heat makes us shiny

and wet), writing descriptions of absent partners,
having a nap, imagining sex (somewhere in Montreal,
with a stranger), killing our parents, munching a cookie

(the Retreat food is divine), swearing (but silently),
swearing some more, tearing up the manuscript
(well, keeping the pieces; the archive might want them),

trying to decide what to wear for the reading tonight,
rewriting the first paragraph (actually, we went for a walk
this afternoon, to that labyrinth down in the coulee)

(looking for inspiration?) (looking for ripe saskatoons?),
(checking now for ticks in our hair) (please, someone,
help), weighing the world's end.

The friars in their chapel bless our failures and ask
St. Francis to go easy on this flock of busy writers.
They finish their prayers. They join us for a glass of wine.

Sharing a Pizza

My daughter Megan and I were in the rain forest
in Costa Rica. We had no names for the things
around us. The birds and the trees were strange,

the myriad nameless insects smacked at our
screened windows like so many hailstones,
the rumours of poisonous snakes made us walk on air.

We dined on guava and breadfruit, on pumpkin soup,
trying to learn new flavours, trying not to be ourselves,
and on the verge of succeeding. We were out of our world:

spiders in their hung webs; howler monkeys alarming us;
ants in red columns around our feet; the bruising cries
of the nearly dead in the strangled trees in the green gloom.

We were dissolving. The songs of the flitting birds
were not songs at all, they were a confusion of discords,
a turmoil of is and not, a warning. But to what? Or to whom?

Travel is not a warning. Travel is a bus ride out of the park.
Travel is an old woman who offers you her seat on the bus.
I had no choice but to sit down, me a white-haired guest.

Megan and I were surprised at the sight of a pizza joint,
there on the trail outside the park gate. We looked at
each other, then nodded. The door was a beaded curtain.

Cheticamp, Cape Breton Island

The novel I haven't finished is finished,
at least for today. Or tomorrow. I gave it to Laura
to read. Laura reads books for a living.

She was making a scallop supper for all of us
there in a house on a shore in a small Acadian village.
Laura likes cooking. We were all of us waiting.

Why would you ask your daughter to read a novel
you couldn't write? Why would you ask
when she was so busy she couldn't say no?

The meal was a success, a marvel. Scallops fresh
from the sea. Snow crab dripping melted butter.
New potatoes. Lip-staining wedges of wild-blueberry pie.

But about the manuscript. Laura placed it on top of the fridge.
I forgot to mention, we were drinking wine,
a delicate white from the Bay of Fundy. And a local beer.

In the morning we went to look for whales, Laura and Megan
and Mike and I. After all, we were on vacation. The lobster
season was over. It would soon be time to trap eels.

It was an in-between season. Laura mentioned as much;
we were on vacation. She was reading to relax.
She had read half the night. It was she who pointed out

a pod of minke whales, frolicking in blue water, under
a headland of rock. Mike spotted an eagle, watching the whales.
We all of us watched the whales and the eagle. We all were happy.

Guesswork

I ransacked my life for a poem. I pillaged my dreams.
I sacked a whole city of books, looking for clues
that would lead to a clue that would solve the riddle.

Lucretius says, of course there are gods; but the gods
are as helpless as we. He doesn't quite say it, but perhaps
we should offer them pity. Done in by creation itself.

I mean the gods. Not us. Well us too.
The gods moved into books. Who wrote the books?
We wrote the books. In whose dream, then, are we dreaming?

Just Be Yourself 1

I finally had a date. The most beautiful girl
in philosophy class. I said to my buddies, What should I do?
I was nervous. They told me, Just be yourself.

I was confounded. How could I manage to be myself?
A solipsism. A circular argument.
A self-proving statement that might be false.

Lucretius had hit it dead on: we are all made up
of atoms. We can't see the atoms of which
we are made. The self is unlikely.

We started with coffee. I shouldn't have mentioned
the impossible self. Not to our basketball star.
She had just won a game by dunking the ball.

She was reading Lucretius. She knew he had said
that love is bad news, a hazard, a sure path to pain.
She had to rush off; she had a paper to write by morning.

Just Be Yourself 2

I wanted to get on with my life's work. I finally
had a job interview. My prospective employer
gave me no clues as to where I should go for the meeting.

I stopped to fill up with gas. The station was self-service.
I tried to ask for directions. There was no one on duty.
I cleaned my windshield. I paid with my credit card.

Who was my prospective employer? That wasn't clear
in the message I'd received. Benefits not guaranteed,
but I might get a bonus. If I kept on performing. At what?

I went to a massage parlour just off Main Street.
Perhaps the masseur could loosen me up. Or at least
give me solace. But the city fathers had closed the place.

What would I be doing? That wasn't clear in the offer.
And what about the interview? I phoned my aunt in Victoria, BC,
the one who reads tea leaves. She counselled me, Just be yourself.

Touch

Why do we so often touch our own faces?
Psychologists have lots of theories. I figure
our fingers are checking for damage.

Chicken pox put a scar on my nose. I was
ten months old and itchy. My face reminds me:
I scratched my own face. I scratch my face now.

Time is a kind of poet, writing three-line stanzas
on the blank above our eyes. We read the lines
with our fingers. We rush to the pharmacy.

It's always too late. I check again, touching
the place where a hockey puck ripped my cheek.
We cherish our scars for their boasting rights.

The wind is a show-off; it rubs the face raw.
The hands can't protect it, try as they might.
The sun lifts a palm to the forehead.

A kiss can ravish the mouth, confound the tongue.
A kiss, that too is a kind of scar; we are certain
the world can read our rejoicing.

We blush. We would hide the blush and don't succeed.
The tell-tale silence brings up the hand.
Joy, the illusionist, feigns a regret.

We are told that age makes our ears grow large. Consider
Buddha. We tug at an earlobe, hoping to be wise.
We stroke our chins. We tickle our noses.

Winter Parka

My winter parka is leaking feathers.
Some days I look like a half-plucked duck.
My winter parka is bulky and red.

Some days I look like the Michelin Man,
ready to explode. Beware the warm sun.
Beware the weatherman's prognostications.

We are all casualties. We rehearse the seasons,
hoping our parkas will melt into green.
We keep a dark space in the storage closet.

Appalachian Back Roads

The fields are turning to forest again, here
in Upstate New York. The squared clearings
grow raggedly new with maple and pine.

The young trees measure our defeat.
It would seem they have been waiting.
The rusted ploughshare transforms into trace.

An archaeologist speculates: They lived in
small, cold houses. The had domesticated cows,
chickens, pigs and horses. They survived chiefly

on the seeds of plants they had learned to grow
in rocky soil on rough and forested hillsides.
They supplemented this with hunting and gathering.

They had developed primitive trade routes and roads.
They seem to have had dance and prayer rituals
in which they consumed transformational drinks.

Hot Fudge Sundae

You have a hot fudge sundae with a friend,
each of you making excuses. You would
never do this if you were alone.

You had no choice, you tell each other,
spooning into the plastic dish, you are
innocence itself. You whisper calories,

but don't agree with statistics; you risk
a cold/hot heresy. Devout non-believers,
accounting appetite, you lick your lips.

Making Faces

All he wants is a new face. He sticks
out his tongue. No one takes note.
He pulls his ears away from his head.

He dresses for Halloween. He wears a mask
and carries a large empty sack. It's
a January night. He receives no treats.

Perhaps the face is a mirage. He feigns
a worried look. No one takes note.
He becomes care-worn and worried.

He tries growing old. His face maps
his terror in delicate lines, a path
to his secret longing. No one takes note.

Driving to the Airport at Five AM

So many lights in the windows of houses.
What happened to sleep? So many cars
lighting the streets of so many houses.

The dark is defeated. We have run out
of dark. We are darkness-deprived.
We rise from the runway, imagining night.

Just for Once

Once upon a time. The lovers had in mind
eternity. They would bluff their way
out of human folly. They would avoid pain.

Once in a blue moon. The lovers coincide
with their own intentions. They take delight
as they find it. They find it in taking delight.

Once is enough. The lovers dissolve
into silence, into Platonic calm; they become
the healed halves of a cracked egg.

Once in a lifetime. The lovers have only
a lifetime. Their bodies rejoice in the tick
of the clock. There is a way to measure now.

Please Post

There WILL be a meeting tonight.
We WILL meet in your bed. Or mine.
You WILL call the meeting to order.

The Agenda: 1) Wanting to get to know you
better, 2) Complex desire, 3) Simple lust,
4) The nature of impatience, 5) Words, words.

Order of Business: We WILL proceed but
not according to schedule. Disorder will rule,
disorder of hands, disorder of pillows.

Next Meeting: Immediately following
that which precedes. Should the sun come up
too early, we WILL go off Daylight Saving.

Arctic Miracle

The Mackenzie's mouth became its own channels.
The beluga whales swam into the delta waters
as if to watch a riverboat wade out to salt sea.

We were going on tow, getting ready to risk the run.
The *Nahanni Jane* had a riverboat's flat bottom.
We were towing barges out onto the Beaufort Sea,

hauling a winter's supplies to Tuktoyaktuk,
flour and fuel and traps and tinned milk
for the Hudson's Bay post and the trappers.

We met a stiff wind. We travelled for hours,
standing still. We were running scared on rough water.
Thank heavens the sun didn't set that night.

Night Vision

We were the boat's crew, safe in a Yellowknife bar.
Someone came in and said, A man just drowned
in the harbour. Could you help the police with the dragging?

It was the end of the shipping season. We were drunk.
The mate turned on the searchlight, its long beam
faintly lighting the black water in the black night.

It was fall and cold and snowing. Like I say,
we were all quite drunk, there in the wheelhouse,
watching. We avoided each other's eyes.

Two zigzag skiffs crossed into the streaked light
and back into darkness, their grappling hooks in tow,
the cops in the skiffs in parkas, bent close to the water

as if to listen, testing the weight on the lines,
on the hooks, watching as if they could read
the black depth, testing the weight on the lines.

Like I say, I was pretty well hammered. Maybe
that's why I cried when they pulled up the body.
It looked perfectly dry, not water but dust.

To Eli Mandel

You liked to read poems aloud to your friends,
and we liked to listen, your quick voice
reading Webb and Atwood, Bowering, Purdy,

you, your quick hands waving the words off the page,
all of us gathered there in Fort San, catching
the edge of creation while down by Echo Lake
the screeching gulls paid no attention,

all of us listening, hearing your voice,
in your voice scorched prairie, the solace of touch,
the rent regions of the heart, the place without place,

all us waiting, knowing you will say,
Now read us a poem, your quick smile
saying, Invent us, quickly, invent us, again.

CJCA, Alberta, 1935

As lonesome as the lonesome train
that whistled in the autumn air,
the hobo self was singing rain,

the rain was falling everywhere,
but mostly in the hobo's mind,
the music of his near despair

was giving hope to his own kind
who hoped somewhere a meal to find
and rode the boxcar in the rain.

Horse's Petunia

When the show host asked, And what
did you learn, riding a buggy to school,
a cutter in winter, staring at a horse's petunia?

I might have answered, of buffalo beans,
or of ducks in the ditches, or of muskrats
dining on cattails, or of orioles nesting,

or I might have mentioned blizzards,
or a heated rock under my boots in the cutter,
or a dead lynx on the road, or the mud,

but instead I said (getting ready to read a poem),
It wasn't time wasted. Now, at least, I know
a horse's ass when I see one.

Pembina Highway, Winnipeg

Drugstores and auto shops for bodily repair.
Beauty salons and pedicures for toenails and hair.
Gas stations and liquor stores to help us getting there.

The devious ways of pleasure. The stop and start.
What is pasted on billboards is our kind of art.
Pedestrians jaywalk. The city buses fart.

The devious ways of beauty. The people in the bars.
The fast food outlets. The even faster cars.
To hell with plastic surgery. We've come to like the scars.

Dear Mark Twain—

Sir, I know you are not Mark Twain, you are
Samuel Langhorne Clemens, of Hannibal, Missouri.
But you are Mark Twain. I have a question.

My wife and I, when we lived in Iowa City,
followed the Mississippi down to your Hannibal.
Yes, I know, you're from Missouri, show me.

A pilgrimage of sorts. We watched the river,
watched for Huck and Jim. Watched for you.
No rafts in sight. The steamboats were for tourists.

We found, in that 1960s town, a white picket fence.
A sign said, Painted by Tom Sawyer. The paint was fresh.
Tell us now, sir, if you will, Who among us is not a fiction?

Flooding the Rink

This morning two men are flooding the rink.
The way they do it is, they have an empty oil drum
on a sled. They fill the drum with heated water,

then pull it out onto to the ice and spill it evenly,
the water melting the ice, the two, the water
and the ice, then fusing in the sub-sub-zero morning.

Tonight, on the new sheet of ice, we boys
will ask the girls to skate. If we find the nerve.
The girls pretend no interest. That helps.

The way you do it is, you skate side by side,
holding hands, your right in the right hand
of your partner, the left in the left.

The lights reflect in the perfect ice.
The open rink is iron cold. We pair off.
We keep our mitts on.

If I Were You

If I were you
what would I do?
I would double my sum.

But if you were me
then who would I be?
And if we became

each other's other
and wanted to kiss,
why then would we bother?

NATION IN PERIL

BANFF ELK GIVES BIRTH TO TOURIST
SUSPECT IN HAND
[SWM, 51. animal lover, likes long walks...]

FINDS LIVE DRAGON IN CEREAL BOX
CUSTOMER DEMANDS REFUND
[SWM, 37, vegan, likes to eat out...]

CANADIAN MALE FAKES ORGASM
WOMEN CLAIM VIOLATION OF RIGHTS
[DWF, 46, professor, likes a good time...]

TORY MP SUPPORTS ARTS
RCMP LAY CHARGES
[SWF. 29, artist, will arrange private showing...]

Freedom of Choice: Pie Shop

Consider, if you will, the raspberry pie,
each berry itself a cluster of tiny berries
that will flood the tongue with pregnant juices, and joy,

or lemon meringue: a quick tang under
beaten egg whites, the meringue itself
browned in the oven, the hot lemon sweet,

or you might take a fancy to apple, dutch apple,
robust and earthy, the apple of, and things
like that, sprinkled with bark from the cinnamon tree,

and coconut cream has its sinful side, a shredded
surprise in the custard slide against the teeth,
a small moustache of pleasure, an invitation.

Anne of Green Gables, **Found Poem**

"She sprang to her feet, her bright fancies
fallen into cureless ruin."
And then he wept, softly, in the pitiless rain.

Wind Chill Factor

Discrepancies abound in the weather.
Tonight she is watching late movies.
He decides to wear his toque to bed.

Thermometers misread the wind.
Beware the exposed throat, the draft.
He wears his toque to breakfast.

Home for lunch, and chilled to the bone.
She is the weather of his love.
He throws all caution to the wind.

About the Author

In a dream last night he forgot
to shovel the walk for the postman.
What message is he expecting?

The sun came up again this morning.
What a miracle!
He sings in the shower.

Today he is sure he will get down to work.
He scrapes the ice off his windshield.
He stops at Starbucks for a latte.

Goose Air Base, USAF

Black trees, pale snow. A Labrador winter night.
The B-52 slid into the forest, missing the runway
by less than a mile. Air Rescue was there in minutes.

It was slow, like a dream, the crew members said,
those who weren't killed. Cold War alert,
they called it. The Korean conflict dragged on.

One of the crew was missing.
They found him four days later, buried in snow.
He had hardly a scratch on him.

He was careful, answering our questions.
It seemed a long time, he said. I died once or twice.
It was his pity for us that made us believe him.

I Swear I Didn't Do It

Somebody stole the St. Christopher medal
that was your travel guide and protector. I didn't do it.
However, I happen to know where the medal got to.

Somebody tore a page out of your mystical meditations,
that entry about how you want to live your nights
like Hildegard of Bingen. Don't blame me.

Somebody anonymous sent you a card,
inviting you out for pasta and wine and confession.
Don't blame me. I swear I didn't do it.

Bad Timing

I asked the dog, What exactly is time?
He misunderstood the question. He wagged
his tail. It was time for me to feed him.

I stopped at a 7-Eleven for my daily
news fix. The cashier had an Indian accent.
I was sure he would know, I asked him simply,

If the universe has no beginning, no end,
how can there be time? I can see, he said,
it's going to be a long day.

I was sitting by this Chinese lady
on the subway train. I thought she might be
a Buddhist. I asked her, casually,

What do you make of eternity?
She didn't respond. I asked again. She answered,
without an accent, I don't speak any English.

There were forty-four seconds left to play
in the football game. Those seconds lasted
eight minutes. I signalled for a time out.

Country Boy

His humour is so sad. Sometimes he is
the boy who seeks out isolation,
but cannot bear to be alone.

His sadness is so funny. Hurtin'
makes him sing, and flirtin'
is his way of putting up a curtain.

Walking Backwards in a Blizzard

It was part of our education, learning
to lean on the wind, trusting the wind,
learning to be the hypotenuse.

Trigonometry, our teacher explained, is the study
of angles. Late for school is a failure
to connect two points with a straight line.

The blizzard sealed our eyes, we said.
We had to walk backwards in order to see—
our tracks in the snow, the shape of the wind.

The past, we argued, must be a curved line.
Walking backwards in the driven snow,
we had arrived, by our calculations, early to class.

I Saw It With My Own Eyes

We were going to Europe by ship.
I looked out the porthole that first night
and saw the black waves lashing the sky.

I got seasick, threw up in the bathroom.
Next morning I said to a deckhand, Quite
a storm. Storm? he said. What storm?

I saw it with my own eyes. I mean,
the storm. My wife hadn't noticed.
Perception, she said, is a misperception.

Later that morning we saw a ship, sailing
above the horizon. It's a mirage I said,
beating her to the draw. She said, Are you sure?

The Word Sprang to My Lips

Perhaps it was an adjective I sought.
But what was I trying to qualify?
Or maybe it was a proper noun.

It wasn't Inuvik. It wasn't Medicine Hat.
It wasn't Madeline or Joe or Stephanie.
It wasn't a river's name, like Amazon or Nile.

It wasn't a smell, like lavender or sage.
It wasn't exactly a taste, but now
we're getting warmer. But it wasn't a taste.

What is it that so confuses the brain?
I didn't know whether to look or not look.
Just then the word sprang to my lips.

Visit to Japan

In the Edo Bar
I bought Hokusai a drink.
You are old, he said.

As for himself, he
was hardly a day over
his two-hundredth year.

I love your landscapes,
I told him, me flushing red.
From the hot sake.

He offered to sell
me a print of Mt Fuji.
The bar was crowded.

Floating world, he said.
Boats. Canals. A wooden bridge.
Right up your alley.

I had to step out.
I peed off a wooden bridge,
into a river.

Cottage Season

The sand and salt that were spread
on the streets are now spread on whatever
it was that was grass. Not a leaf in sight.

Rivers explode. We call it spring.
Robins come back; they build their nests
in blowing snow. Enough already.

Things aren't looking up. We can't resist
a greenhouse visit. We plant tomatoes.
One frosty night we forget to cover them.

We open the cottage. Ice busted the pump.
The plumber is booked through July.
Everything seems the physical shits.

We fill a closet with winter clothes.
Our bodies come out of the dark.
We bask in the sun, insanely happy.

"no ideas but in things"

Making meaning is easy enough,
but making the meaning mean is tough.
I am not (quite) a convert to truth,

nor to eye for eye, nor tooth for tooth.
I'd rather a rhyme that gives relief
than pie in the sky that gives belief.

Ideas are things, Doc Williams said.
He was a poet. Now he's dead.
Desire done with, appetites fed.

Seduction Attempt 1

Too busy to send me a message. You.
Yet you went to the store for red wine.
Something you read about your heart.

Good. Great. May you live forever.
Like Tiresias. Getting older by the day.
Older and older. Those ointments you rub

onto your nipples, into the hairs on your belly,
onto your buttocks, down between your warm thighs—
they won't keep you young.

Don't you get it? You could give me a call,
or send me an e-mail. I've heard of a cure for aging.
It will only take an hour of your time.

Seduction Attempt 2

I have this new sex toy. I think you'll like it.
It actually talks. No kidding, I mean it.
I've tried it myself. It actually talks.

You might want to bring your own pillow.
This new item whispers more than it talks.
Though it can be persuaded to give out a cry.

And another thing: it likes conversation.
Questions about forever or now. About
a quick drink. About a late breakfast.

If I'm not at home when you arrive,
just climb into my bed. This new sex toy
will be in the closet. Just say, Hello. I'm here.

Applause

I hired this guy to lead the applause at my readings.
He seemed a sensitive person. He wrote a few poems
himself. I should have known better.

I read of my pain, of my sorrows. My failed love affairs,
my bad investments, my bladder problems.
He led the crowd in gales of laughter.

I read a few poems on the joys in my life. My various
happy marriages, my arts grants, my reading tour of the USSR.
Half the room burst into tears.

My clapper read a few poems of his own composition.
Tedious things. Pathetic. Poems about truth and justice.
To my surprise, the listeners feigned approval.

I saw the plain truth then. He was a snake in the weeds,
a swine's curly tail, a donkey's dong, an ass's rectum.
Why should we forgive our enemies?

Pessoa and His Heteronyms

We were seated for drinks with a statue:
Fernando Pessoa himself, cast in bronze,
at a bronze table, there in a square in Lisbon.

We were seated on bronze chairs,
out-of-doors, my two daughters and I.
We were waiting for table service.

Meg asked Pessoa if he'd like a coffee.
He was rather stiff and formal, in his bronze hat.
He wouldn't nod; he wouldn't speak a word.

Laura said to Pessoa, My dad likes your poems.
He thinks you're the greatest. He says
when he first read you, he fell off his chair.

Pessoa didn't so much as crack a smile.
It was one of his many voices that spoke.
From the empty chair I was sitting on.

Sir, the voice said, I am and am not
Pessoa. Make up your own mind. Meanwhile,
get off my lap, you're squashing me.

Cars Whizzing By

This a landscape poem. The cars
are going somewhere. You can tell
by the pulsing sound; they're in a hurry.

You can tell by the smell of burnt gasoline.
The cars have intention. They have freedom
of will. They are going somewhere.

You can tell by the slash of headlights,
the blur of tires and licence numbers.
There are no drivers to be seen.

Henri Rousseau, "The Sleeping Gypsy"

They called him fantastical, naïve.
In his painting the gypsy is sleeping;
she is sleeping beside her mandolin.

In the painting the curious lion
puts his nose to the sleeper.
The moon is bright and full.

You are (not) the full moon.
You are (not) the intrigued lion.
You are (not) the sleeping gypsy.

There's a jar by the mandolin.
Perhaps the jar contains cool water.
A desert contains the jar, the dream.

Terracotta Army

The third soldier in the third row
of the thousands of ranked clay soldiers
in the excavations outside Xian

looked exactly like the guide who was explaining:
There is a world below the world, a garden of the dead;
there is, in this necropolis, a dream of living

after having lived. The man who united China
proposed to escape death's little boundary.
Qin Shi Huang. He proposed to rule in the afterlife.

Our guide was going on: These soldiers
have stood at attention for two thousand years.
Once they were terrifying. Now they are beautiful.

Our guide looked exactly like one of the soldiers,
except, he was wearing a black cowboy hat.
He was a fan of American movies.

Laundering the Poem

I wrote the idea on a serviette;
I put the serviette in my shirt pocket;
I put the shirt, and the serviette,

in the washing machine, along with the usual
measure of liquid Tide. So far so good.
I put the wet shirt in the dryer. Fair enough.

The shirt came out dry and clean. So did
the serviette. So did my memory of the idea
I had put on the serviette and into the pocket

of my shirt and into the washing machine
and into the dryer. I just want the censors to know.
At last, I have written a clean poem.

Dear Lovelorn,

You must buck up. You say she called you
a fine sort of prize. Maybe she meant it.
You must have more faith in language.

You need a better self-image. A bit more bluster.
And why did you send that e-mail?
You must learn to think twice.

True, she may have found a new lover.
Another man's socks on the floor by her bed
is not a good sign. But appearances are deceiving.

The human brain is easily fooled.
Your question is one of cause and effect.
You must not jump to conclusions.

You must buy some new clothes.
How old is your tie collection?
Politicians, remember, like to wear red.

And please, no more home videos.
Some contests aren't worth winning.
You must get hold of yourself.

Horoscope

Thank your lucky stars. Today
you might win the lottery. Chances are
you didn't buy a ticket, but if you had

you might have struck it rich; today
you might meet a gorgeous widow, but
the chances are you haven't combed your hair.

The Crab is your symbol. You like deep water.
The moon is your planet. You are mooning around.
In your miserable way, you are happy.

Today you might have written a poem.
But the chances are you've a hangover.
There. You've connected with the cosmos.

Café au Lait and Croissants in Strasbourg

Simone Vauthier, geraniums, red tile roofs; we discuss Canlit,
French Resistance and her heroic father, my great-grandmother
Teresia Tschirhart, born just down the road, emigrating.

We discuss the staying, the going away; how make choices?
The man at home, concealed in the forest. The woman, closing
and locking the door. Which way the inside, which way the out?

We are having croissants and café au lait, Simone and I,
discussing narrative tangle, on her balcony, near the cathedral.
She refills three cups. Who is the third person at the table?

Daedalus

The brain, we are told, is plastic; it can make new routes
when troubles arise. A stroke. A fall. Shrapnel in the head.
A birth defect. The discourse of memory. The ruts of the past.

It can make new routes, the brain. Connections. It finds
new plots for the stories of old. Yes, I am not in love.
War is the great inventor. Spring will surprise us early.

You've been reading my brain again. Have you noticed
the changes? I now eat bananas, even though they give me hives.
I can smell the coffee brewing, but I only want one cup.

Hope has taken the form of the brain itself. It is the brain
that builds toward heaven. So what if the airplane crashes?
At least we dared, in this new way, to reach for the sun.

The Feet of the Lone Traveller

The sound of his shoes on the cobbled street is the sound
of his shoes on the cobbled street. He says he is not a pilgrim.
The tourists are safe in Gaudi's church, a dream of the sacred city.

Barcelona is dark, in the almost night. The harbour street
smells of a harbour's wreckage. The Columbus statue
is wet and crying after the rain. And again it is raining.

The sound of his shoes on the cobbled street comes back
from the walls of the shops and apartments. Perhaps Columbus,
in his need to depart, was weary of shops and apartments.

The sound of the shoes of the traveller slows. His feet are sore
with all his walking. Does not a pilgrimage wear out your feet?
He stops. He wants to speak. He has just come by to say hello.

Living Life as a Poet

I hope I can resist. It's a stupid idea.
What I was thinking was,
I could buy an estate in the Florida Keys,

mix with the Hemingway look-alikes.
I'd have to grow my beard longer.
Too bad I'm a little short of cash.

I suppose I could rent a house
somewhere on the Mexican coast.
They say the prices are right,

if you don't mind the drug wars.
I can say please in Spanish. *Por favor*.
Too bad my stomach can't take jalapenos.

I suppose I could borrow a tent
from one of my camping friends.
A summer on Lake Athabasca.

Not too close to the tar sands.
Commune with nature. Poach a moose.
Too bad I'm afraid of guns.

Well, finally, I suppose I could just stay put
where I am, drink coffee, rewrite this poem.
What a stupid idea. I hope I can resist.

Don't Blame Us

Chances are we'll have a cold winter.
We had a warm fall. You know how things work.
Nature's balance: Paying Peter to rob Paul.

Chances are the Blue Jays won't win the World Series.
It's not in the cards. The odds are against it.
You can't win for losing. Don't even try.

Chances are we've run out of luck. Time
will tell. You know that cows come home
for milking. Chickens come home to roost.

Chances are the world will end. Don't worry.
Fossil fuels in constant flame. You know
who it was lit the fires. It was the Martians.

Victorian Lit, University of Alberta, 1946

Professor Jones said we should listen
to what he was saying instead of writing it down.
We wrote that down too. What he was saying.

We were studying Matthew Arnold's "Dover Beach."
Half the students in the class were freshly back from war.
One of the veterans asked, When did Arnold write this poem?

Perhaps he hadn't been paying attention. I checked my notes
and read the dates: commenced 1851, published 1867.
Professor Jones said, Every enduring poem was written today.

I Try to Steal My Identity

Some hackers show me how. I break into the system.
My date of birth must be in error. It says I was born
in a century past. In a time that no one remembers.

It says I was born in a homesteader's shack
on virgin prairie. But there is no virgin prairie.
No one remembers a crocus spring.

There are no orioles in the trees. There is
no horsehair for their nests. There are no boys
with slingshots, trying to scare the sun.

We like telling stories to the young, but the young
don't like to listen. It is their refusing to hear
that gives new syllables to their tongues.

The kids now play with computers. They show me,
Here, hack into your life. But there must be an error.
The rising sun, back then, was an oriole colour.

Playing Cards With My Sisters

My sister Pat brings out a bag of nickels
and two decks of cards. Before we sit
to the table she starts to deal.

We each have a sip of brandy or wine.
Kay likes to sit to my left. She knows
I will make useful discards.

I can't keep track of what's been played.
My sisters can talk and play and drink and count,
all at the same time. Jane says, Pay attention.

We laugh together. Pay up, they tell me,
You lost. Again. We laugh together.
I'm the luckiest player. I'm paying attention.

Nature Buff

I thought buff meant naked. As in, in the buff.
Why can't words mean what they say?
I went ahead and took off my clothes.

I was alone on a Mexican beach. I was being
a kind of holy hermit, a metaphysician of nature.
I'd immerse myself in the welcoming sea.

Two Mexican cops rode up over a dune
on two Mexican horses. One of them pointed
(the cops that is, not the horses) at my private parts.

They (again, the gun-toting cops) guessed I was
(though I didn't have a stitch on) English-speaking.
One of them pointed at the welcoming sea.

Dick, he said. Dink. Don't enter the water
this time of year. He doffed his hat before
spurring his horse. The sharks are *hambriento*.

My Windshield Scraper

Canadian cold, this weather,
and I didn't plug in my car last night,
and ice formed and snow fell till morning;

so why in hell can't someone invent
a windshield scraper that will scrape
on its own, the weather be damned;

but no, a brush at one end, a blade at the other,
something the Cro-Magnon crowd might have
made overnight, if they'd had Hondas;

so now I'm freezing my technological
fingers off, blinded by freezing tears,
stiff in every frozen joint and muscle,

warmed only by old men's mutterings:
Cold as a well digger's ass.
Freeze the nuts off an iron bridge.

Locating Story

Tell me the truth, his mother said.
Her breath was short, her face was red.
He hauled himself out from under his bed.

Tell me the truth, his mother said.
He might have told a lie instead.
Better the truth be left unsaid.

My story lies in between, he said,
in the shadows under my bed,
under the covers, in my head.

Late Breaking News

Pheidippides, the messenger, after the Battle
of Marathon, ran flat-out those twenty-six miles to Athens;
We have won, he gasped, then fell, then died.

The news is always breaking. Even the good news
breaks our bodies. Athens: the city saved.
490 BCE: some call it the birth of our civilization.

Six thousand four hundred Persians: dead.
How can death be news? Who gave the count
to their Persian homes? How did they do it without TV?

Making an Impression

I was standing still when I fell off my feet.
No, I was coming out of a bar on Corydon.
No, I hit a patch of black ice on campus.

No, I was walking down the cathedral steps.
No, actually, I was brushed by a speeding car.
To be perfectly honest, this big guy pushed me.

You've got to appreciate my predicament.
I'm a ghost. No one can see me until
it's too late. Lying in the snow

I'm an imprint. An indentation.
Lying in the snow I'm an absence
that anyone should recognize as me.

Cockadoodledoo

Dogs bark. Cats meow. Cows moo.
Pigs oink. Horses whinny or neigh.
What in the world do humans do?

Crows caw. Cocks crow. We like to say
that robins sing, which might be true.
Does what we think we hear lead us astray?

We humans cannot really oink or meow.
Consider then a mooing pig, a singing crow,
a barking cat, or possibly a neighing cow.

Watching for Signs

The ripping tides of autumn ride the sand.
The seagulls twist the wind, the albatross
departs the shore and any scent of land.

The walker walks the beach, condemns the sea
for all that is unseen, observes the loss,
the line of empty shells, the driftwood tree.

Nothing is that nothing is. The fish,
presumably, are being fish, the moss
is mossy moss, the wish a wishy wish.

What is is, and what is not is not.
The lucent ocean waves that lift and toss
are not enough to fill the walker's thought.

About Poetic Despair

I offer these lines to poetic death.
They are trying to picture a trotting horse.
They are short by a foot and out of breath.

As for the horse, it is pulling a hearse.
And as for the hearse, it carries a wreath.
The wreath is the sign of a vanishing worth.

The wreath was to honour the living poem.
The wreath is composed of laurel leaf.
No one would claim it as his/her own.

About Poetic Hope

Before I forget: you should know:
he was a metaphysician of before.
We are agreed at least on that: he was

a scholar of what was: a garden wet
with morning dew, wet with creation,
birth, and black with a murder of crows;

before you reach conclusions, consider this:
he was mostly unaware most of the time,
but, even so, we are agreed, spring was worth it.

Grade Ten Typing Lesson: how now brown cow

How might we define cow? A cow is a cow.
And even that is debatable. The adult female
of moose, of elephant, of seal: each is a cow.

Don't be cowed by the question. A cow
eats grass. Except for the adult female
that is moose, elephant, seal or whale.

A cow is a mammal. How could we fail
to notice: the teats, the milk, the tail.
But how know a mare is not a cow?

The male of cattle can also be cow,
as any cowboy will tell you: check under the tail
for particulars. How now brown cow?

The Sky is Falling

The meadowlarks sing
haiku on prairie fence posts:
barbed wire notations.

The goldfinches flash
tropical in northern air.
Where did the light go?

The gophers dig holes
and hide in a prairie field.
We feed them poison.

What about coyotes?
They are moving into town.
They like to eat dogs.

And as for people,
well, we claim to like nature.
We make the sky fall.

Everything Considered

The table is rectangular, the ten chairs are functional.
A slippage in category here. The table is functional.
The chairs are not rectangular. What's for lunch?

Today we are having rice and chicken soup.
Or chicken and rice. The breadboard is rectangular.
The cutting edge of the bread knife is a saw.

The loaf of bread keeps changing shape.
The table is elbow-high to someone sitting in a chair.
The knife, it might be suggested, is a magician.

But observe, it is we who make the bread disappear.
The knife remains on the breadboard. The soup
is followed by a lettuce salad. The breadboard

remains on the table. Everything has a function,
but only just. The bread has disappeared.
The empty chairs are arranged as a rectangle.

Time to Spare

By the time I say the word now it's then.
So then, I might ask, what is now?
To answer that question I bought a horse.

How could I keep a horse in my house?
To answer that question I bought a ranch.
Then I decided the house had to go.

Now I live with a horse in a pasture.
I have time to consider what was and is.
By the time I speak the word then it's now.

The future will name itself on arrival.
Right now I am waiting. Just simply waiting.
My horse, in a month, hasn't spoken a word.

The Unnameable

He called his thing his thing.
What a thing to call your thing.
Thing, in a way, is nothing.

He called his dork his dork.
Too bad it rhymes with cork.
He was, himself, a dork.

Doohickey. Try rhyming that
with hockey. Or with softball bat.
Or hickey. Or with rat-a-tat-tat.

Another name for tool is tool.
Life's little push and pull.
Too bad it rhymes with fool.

He called his dink his dink.
He said it liked to bonk.
Too bad it couldn't think.

Motion Sickness

The planet is turning too fast.
I hardly get to bed when it's time to wake up.
I hardly wake up when it's time to go to bed.

The planet has a slight wobble.
It gives me trouble when I'm walking the dog.
I can feel it when I'm climbing a hill.

And what about the oceans,
being jerked around by the moon?
How's a person to get any rest?

Even the dead come back to shake us.
Just this morning I saw my grandmother,
trying to ride a bicycle. Her shroud

got caught in a wheel. She lost her balance.
She fell. I rushed to help her. To my surprise,
I too was on a bicycle. I couldn't stop it.

Noosa Heads, Queensland

The parrots were making a fuss in the top of the tree
just there beyond our balcony. We were way high up.
I said to you, I think they're talking. Those parrots.

I think you're dreaming, you said. No, really, I said,
it's just the Aussie accent, it isn't always clear.
If so, you said, they're telling you something.

The morning was red to orange. The parrots were green.
They were talking. Parrots can talk, I'm sure. I was dreaming
we could stay forever in the canopy, you and I and the parrots.

Risking It

Step into the flowerbed. Paint that museum wall
a new shade of earth. And that art exhibition:
put in your gilded baby shoes, a glass

of water, that sliver from the true cross
that you bought in Hong Kong, a painting
by Norval Morrisseau. Tell us how

you almost cut off your big toe.
Argue against the charms of immortal life.
Practice dancing the Highland fling.

Risk it, dear reader. Looked at, from
night's perspective, your toothbrush is a dream.
Your old leather coat will outlast you,

hanging safe, as it does, on a closet hanger.
Salami will come to give you heartburn.
Celebrate today's pizza as a work of art.